GETTING TO KNOW THE WORLD'S GREATEST
INVENTORS **&** SCIENTISTS

BENJAMIN
FRANKLIN

Electrified the World with New Ideas

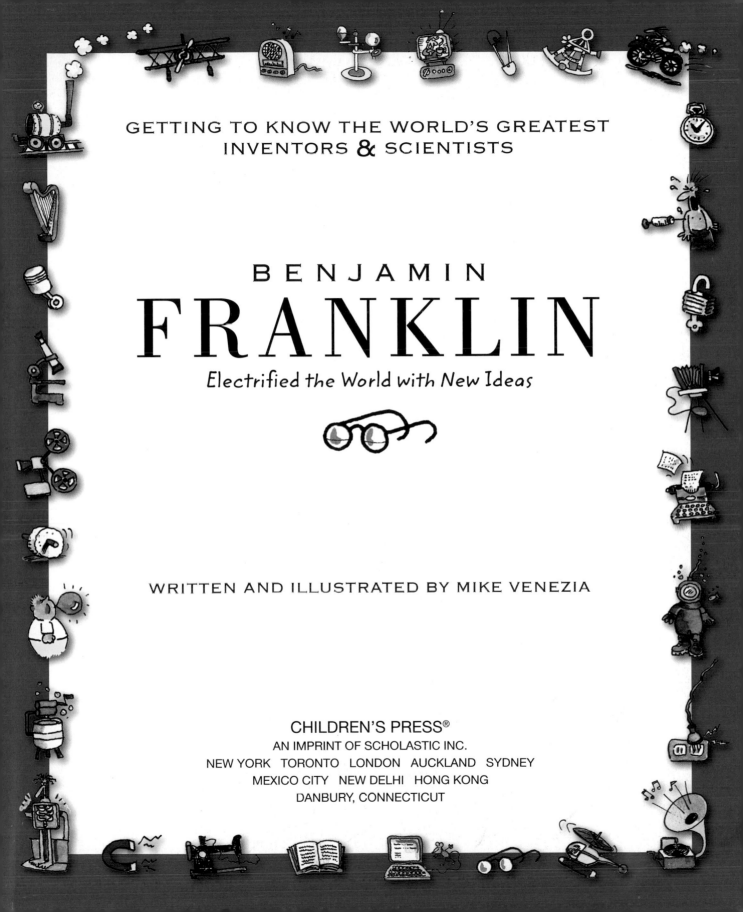

WRITTEN AND ILLUSTRATED BY MIKE VENEZIA

CHILDREN'S PRESS®
AN IMPRINT OF SCHOLASTIC INC.
NEW YORK TORONTO LONDON AUCKLAND SYDNEY
MEXICO CITY NEW DELHI HONG KONG
DANBURY, CONNECTICUT

Reading Consultant: Nanci R. Vargus, Ed.D., Assistant Professor, School of Education, University of Indianapolis

Science Consultant: Doug Welch, Ph.D., McMaster University, Hamilton, Ontario

Photographs © 2010: age fotostock/Ted Wilcox: 30; Art Resource, NY: 3 (Ann Ronan Picture Library, London/HIP); Bridgeman Art Library International Ltd., London/New York: 22 (Archangel Palace, Moscow, Russia), 18 (Collection of the New-York Historical Society, USA); Corbis Images: 23 (Bettmann), 31 (Philadelphia Museum of Art); Getty Images/John Lund: 7; Library Company of Philadelphia/David A. Gentry: 25; NEWSCOM, courtesy of Jane Gitlin's "Fireplace": 20; North Wind Picture Archives: 11; The Bakken Library and Museum, Minneapolis: 6 bottom right; The Granger Collection, New York: 6 left, 10, 14, 16, 19, 24, 29; The Image Works/SSPL: 6 top, 28.

Colorist for illustrations: Andrew Day

Library of Congress Cataloging-in-Publication Data

Venezia, Mike.
  Benjamin Franklin : electrified the world with new ideas / written and illustrated by Mike Venezia.
      p. cm. — (Getting to know the world's greatest inventors and scientists)
  Includes index.
  ISBN-13: 978-0-531-23701-4 (lib. bdg.) 978-0-531-20775-8 (pbk.)
  ISBN-10: 0-531- 23701-X (lib. bdg.)   0-531-20775-7 (pbk.)
  1. Franklin, Benjamin, 1706-1790—Juvenile literature. 2. Inventors—United States—Biography—Juvenile literature. 3. Scientists—United States—Biography—Juvenile literature. 4. Statesmen—United States—Biography—Juvenile literature. 5. Printers—United States—Biography—Juvenile literature. I. Title. II. Series.

  E302.6.F8V46 2009
  973.3'092—dc22
  [B]
                                   2009000305

Benjamin Franklin was a man of many talents and interests. He was a printer, writer, inventor, scientist, diplomat, and Founding Father of the United States of America.

Benjamin Franklin was one of the world's greatest inventors, scientists, and political leaders. He was born in Boston, Massachusetts, in 1706. At that time, Massachusetts was a British colony, ruled by England. When Ben grew up, he would help Massachusetts and twelve other colonies become a new country—the United States of America.

In a way, helping to create the United States was one of Ben's most important inventions. When the United States was being formed, most nations were governed by kings or queens. These powerful people could make up their own laws and could stay in power for as long as they lived. Some of these rulers were unfair, or even cruel, to their citizens.

Ben Franklin became part of a group of remarkable leaders who helped the colonies rebel against the king of England. They formed a different kind of government for the colonies, called a **democracy.** Under this system, everyday citizens would be able to choose their leaders and decide which laws would work best for them.

For most people, helping form a new nation would have been a once-in-a-lifetime accomplishment. But for Ben Franklin, being one of America's Founding Fathers was just one of many achievements. Ben also ran a successful printing business. He was a best-selling author. He founded the University of Pennsylvania and the first public lending library in America.

Like many people, Ben Franklin needed one pair of glasses for reading and another for seeing things in the distance. Frustrated that he constantly had to switch from one pair to the other, he invented bifocals. Bifocals hold both types of lenses in one set of eyeglasses.

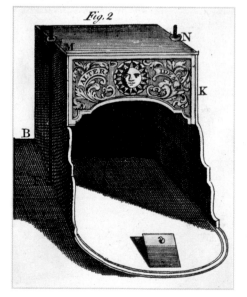

During Franklin's time, fireplaces warmed most people's homes. But fireplaces could be dangerous, and they used lots of wood. Ben invented the Franklin stove (left), a furnace that was safer and more efficient.

Franklin invented the armonica (right). This musical instrument produces beautiful sounds when a player touches the edges of spinning glass bowls with wet fingers.

Ben Franklin became deputy postmaster general for the thirteen colonies and held other important government jobs. Ben came up with all kinds of useful inventions, too, including **bifocal** eyeglasses, a new type of furnace, a musical instrument called an **armonica,** and the **lightning rod.** His experiments with electricity made him one of the most important scientists of the day.

Another Franklin invention was the lightning rod, a metal rod attached to the top of a building to protect it from lightning damage. Lightning is drawn to the rod and is then sent into the ground, where it can do no harm. This important invention is still used today (right).

Ben Franklin grew up in a huge family. He was the fifteenth of seventeen children! Ben's father owned a soap-and-candle making shop in Boston. Mr. Franklin could afford to send Ben to school for only two years. When Ben was ten, he went to work in his father's shop. Ben did just fine learning on his own, though. Whenever he had extra money, he bought books. He loved to read, and educated himself by reading every book he could find. Sometimes Ben rewrote the stories he had read to see if he could make them better.

Ben wasn't crazy about working in the shop. The animal fat used to make soap and candles smelled terrible. Plus, Ben thought it was really boring work.

As a boy, Ben (at right) worked as an apprentice in his brother's printing shop.

Ben's father understood his son's lack of interest in the candle-and-soap business. He arranged for twelve-year-old Ben to work as an **apprentice** to his older brother, James. James was starting up his own print shop in Boston.

Ben liked the idea of printing. He was happy to do anything related to making books and other reading materials. Ben quickly learned to set **type** and operate a printing press. Even as a young teenager, Ben started to become a better printer than James.

This illustration shows young Ben Franklin carrying cases full of type while working for his brother James.

As James's business grew, he decided to start publishing a newspaper. It was called *The New England Courant*. Ben was excited. He offered to help James by writing articles for the paper. But James wouldn't hear of it. He told Ben he was too young to know what he was doing.

Ben figured out a way to get around James's stubborn attitude. He began to write letters to the newspaper, signing them with a made-up name: Mrs. Silence Dogood. Silence was supposedly a middle-aged woman who had humorous thoughts and opinions about life in the colonies.

Ben would write his letters and then slip them under the print shop door at night. When James found the letters in the morning, he'd print them. He thought Silence Dogood's letters were great. So did his readers. James never suspected his brother for a moment.

James (left) was cruel to his brother Ben (right). Eventually, Ben ran away to Philadelphia.

Finally, Ben told James about Silence Dogood. Instead of being thankful, James exploded with anger. He said Ben had tricked him.

Working for James was a pretty miserable experience. Not only was James jealous of Ben, he often beat him. In 1723, seventeen-year-old Ben Franklin decided to run away from home and look for a printing job somewhere else. To gather enough money to leave Boston, he sold all the books he had collected.

Ben ended up settling in Philadelphia, Pennsylvania. When he arrived, he was broke, hungry, and exhausted. He had stuffed extra clothes in his coat, and he spent his last few coins to buy three big, puffy bakery rolls. He walked into town with one roll under each arm as he ate the third one. A girl he passed by chuckled at his appearance. Her name was Deborah Read. Neither Deborah nor Ben could have guessed it, but a few years later they would meet and fall in love.

Ben and Deborah became a couple in 1730. By that time, Ben had worked at a number of printing shops and had enough experience to start his own printing business.

Ben always enjoyed having his family around while he worked. Ben had a son, William, from a previous relationship. He also had two children with Deborah: Francis and Sally. Ben kept as busy as could be, printing a newspaper, official paper money for the colonies, voting ballots, advertisements, and tons of other items.

Ben's most successful project was writing and printing *Poor Richard's Almanack*. An **almanac** is a book that comes out once a year. It's filled with useful facts and information, like weather predictions and dates of **lunar eclipses**. Ben also added his own stories and sayings to the almanac, many of which are still popular today.

Ben (center) working in his printing shop

The almanac was supposedly written by Richard Saunders, another character Ben made up. People all over the colonies loved Richard's short stories and sayings. Ben sold so many copies of the almanac every year that he became a rich man.

As busy as Ben Franklin was, he always found time to improve his city. Ben brought groups of citizens together to make plans for paving Philadelphia's muddy streets. He also formed the city's first hospital and fire department, as well as the first public library in America. People respected Ben's intelligence, logical solutions to problems, and fun personality.

The Library Company of Philadelphia, which Ben Franklin founded, was the first public lending library in America.

As this photograph shows, modern versions of the Franklin stove are still used today.

Ben also found time to come up with inventions. One was the **Franklin stove**. Ben had always noticed that much of the heat from a fireplace was lost as it went up and out the chimney. Ben decided to build an iron stove that stuck out further into the room.

Ben's stove could warm an entire room, and it used less wood than a regular fireplace. Ben's invention worked so well that this type of stove became a major way to heat homes for almost two hundred years.

Ben did an amazing thing after inventing his stove. He decided not to get a **patent** for it. A patent is a legal document that gives an inventor the right to be the only person to make or sell an invention. Ben generously allowed anyone who wanted to copy his stove to go right ahead and do so. He was happy to let other people use his idea to help make their lives more comfortable.

In 1745, Ben began experimenting with electricity. At that time, hardly anyone knew what electricity was or where it came from. But there were some scientific entertainers in the 1700s who put on electricity shows. These showmen used **static electricity** to make sparks jump off people's hands and feet. They could jolt entire groups of people at the same moment or make someone's hair stand on end.

An electrical entertainer putting on a show in the 1700s

Static electricity is electricity that builds up on people or objects when they rub against other objects. This man's hair is standing on end because he has created static electricity by rubbing the metal ball.

Static electricity is the kind of electricity that's created when you slide your feet across a carpet and then touch a doorknob. You can feel the zap and sometimes even see a spark. Ben became very interested in electricity after seeing an electrical show. He was sure electricity was something that could be used for more than just tricks.

Franklin doing an electrical experiment in his lab in 1747

Ben bought some equipment from an electrical entertainer whose show he had seen. He set up a laboratory in his home. He also exchanged letters with other people interested in electricity to learn about their experiences.

Ben Franklin was the first person to use such terms as "positive," "negative," and "charge" when talking about electricity. Ben often made his own electrical equipment for experimenting. He invented one of the first **generators** to create static electricity.

Ben designed and used this electrostatic generator to create static electricity.

Once, Ben did an experiment to show the power of electricity. He decided to have a barbecue for his friends. The main course would be a turkey that was to be killed by an electrical shock.

Unfortunately, after building up a large electrical charge, Ben accidentally touched the wrong wires and was knocked out cold by the jolt!

Ben's flub, however, didn't stop him from doing his most famous experiment: his kite experiment. During the 1700s, many people believed that lightning was a mysterious power that God sent to punish evil people. They didn't think lightning had anything to do with electricity. Ben thought that lightning was the same thing as electricity, and he set out to prove it.

Ben thought that storm clouds contained electrical charges and that these charges sometimes resulted in lightning. He decided to try to draw an electrical charge from a storm cloud to see if he was right.

Ben never meant to attract actual lightning, as most people think. He knew that attracting lightning was terribly dangerous—and could even be fatal.

In 1752, Ben and his son William flew a kite during a thunderstorm. Ben attached a metal wire to the tip of the kite to attract an electrical charge from a storm cloud. Then he attached a brass key to the kite string near the ground.

Ben's kite came close enough to a storm cloud for an electrical charge to travel into the metal rod, down the rain-soaked string, and into the brass key. Ben could feel the electrical charge. He was able move the charge from the brass key into a **Leyden jar,** a simple device that could store static electricity.

A Leyden jar

This illustration shows Franklin's famous kite experiment of 1752.

Ben was thrilled that he was able to charge up the Leyden jar the same way he had done with static electricity from his generator. The electrical charge from the storm cloud was indeed electricity. This meant that lightning was electricity, too.

Ben Franklin probably never dreamed that his early electrical experiments would someday lead to cities being powered by electricity.

It would take almost fifty years before scientists figured out how to get electricity to flow continuously through wires so that it could be used as a source of power. But Ben Franklin's experiments helped pave the way toward the modern use of electricity.

Ben loved experimenting with electricity. He hoped to do more of it. But in the late 1700s, the thirteen colonies' problems with England started demanding his attention. Ben became an important leader during the fight for independence. He went to Europe to represent the colonies. He persuaded the English government to repeal the Stamp Act, an unfair tax on the colonists. He helped write the Declaration of Independence, negotiated the peace treaty with England that ended the Revolutionary War, and took part in the Constitutional Convention that approved the U.S. Constitution.

Ben Franklin spent the rest of his life working to make sure the new United States of America got off

to a good start. He lived a long, colorful life. Ben Franklin died in Philadelphia in 1790 at the age of eighty-four.

Artist Benjamin West painted this heroic painting of Benjamin Franklin drawing electricity from the sky.

Glossary

almanac (AWL-muh-nak) A book, published once a year, that includes facts about a wide variety of subjects

apprentice (uh-PREN-tiss) Someone who learns a trade or craft by working with a skilled person

armonica (ahr-MON-ih-kuh) A musical instrument that uses a series of glass bowls to produce musical tones when they are rubbed

bifocals (BYE-foh-kuhlz) Eyeglasses that have one section for seeing things that are up close and another for seeing things in the distance

democracy (di-MOK-ruh-see) A way of governing a country in which the people choose their leaders in elections

Franklin stove (FRANK-lin STOHV) A cast-iron stove for heating a room

generator (JEN-uh-ray-tur) A device that converts mechanical energy—such as that made by a hand winding a crank—into electrical energy

Leyden jar (LYE-din JAHR) A device used to store an electrical charge

lightning rod (LITE-ning ROD) A metal rod attached to an exposed part of a tall structure to send lightning harmlessly into the ground

lunar eclipse (LOO-nur i-KLIPS) The passage of Earth between the sun and the moon, so that all or part of the moon's light is blocked out

patent (PAT-uhnt) A legal document giving an inventor the sole right to manufacture or sell an invention

static electricity (STAT-ik i-lek-TRISS-uh-tee) An electrical charge that builds up on the surface of a material due to friction

type (TIPE) Small pieces of metal with raised letters or numbers on their surfaces; used when printing with a printing press

Index